QED WordBank

Learning Words with Monsters

ZIA'S Colours

First published in the UK in 2005 by
QED Publishing
A Quarto Group company
226 City Road
London EC1V 2TT
www.qed-publishing.co.uk

A Catalogue record for this book is available from the British Library.

ISBN 1 84538 253 6

Written by Wendy Body
Designed by Alix Wood
Editor Hannah Ray
Illustrated by Sanja Rescek

Series Consultant Anne Faundez
Publisher Steve Evans
Creative Director Louise Morley
Editorial Manager Jean Coppendale

Printed and bound in China

QED WordBank

Learning Words with Monsters

ZIA'S Colours

Wendy Body

QED Publishing

QED

I'm drawing a **circle** and making it **pink**.
What am I painting here, do you think?

pink circle

5

I've put **spikes** on the circle
and coloured them **brown**
and on top of one **spike**,
there's a **yellow crown**.

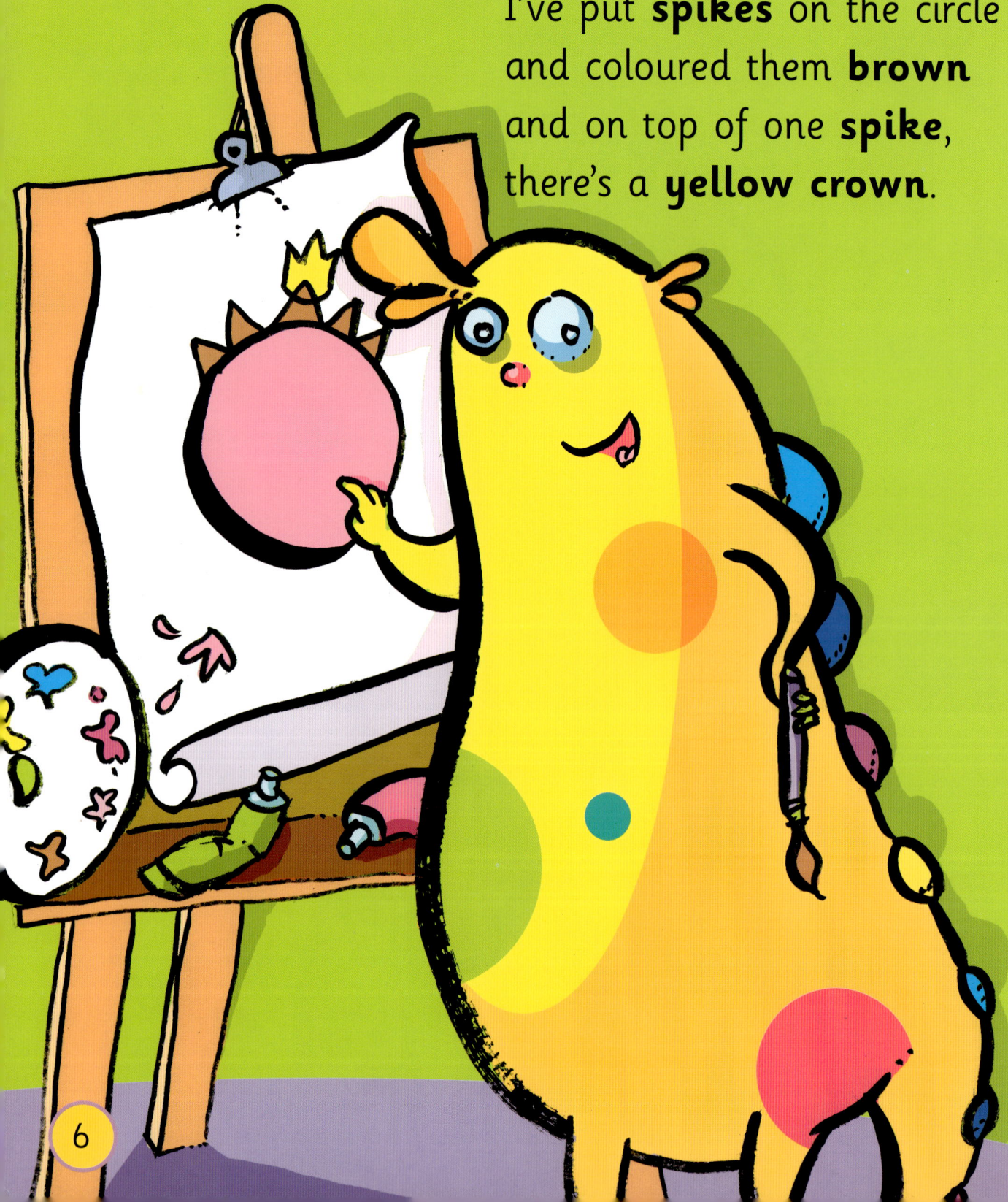

yellow crown

brown spike

With one **blue mouth** and **eyes** that are **red**,
my circle's become the Monster King's head!

red eye

blue mouth

9

Now I'm drawing a **square** and making it **grey**.
What am I painting here, would you say?

10

grey square

I've made the sky dark to show that it's night, and I'm painting **stars white** to make them look bright.

white star

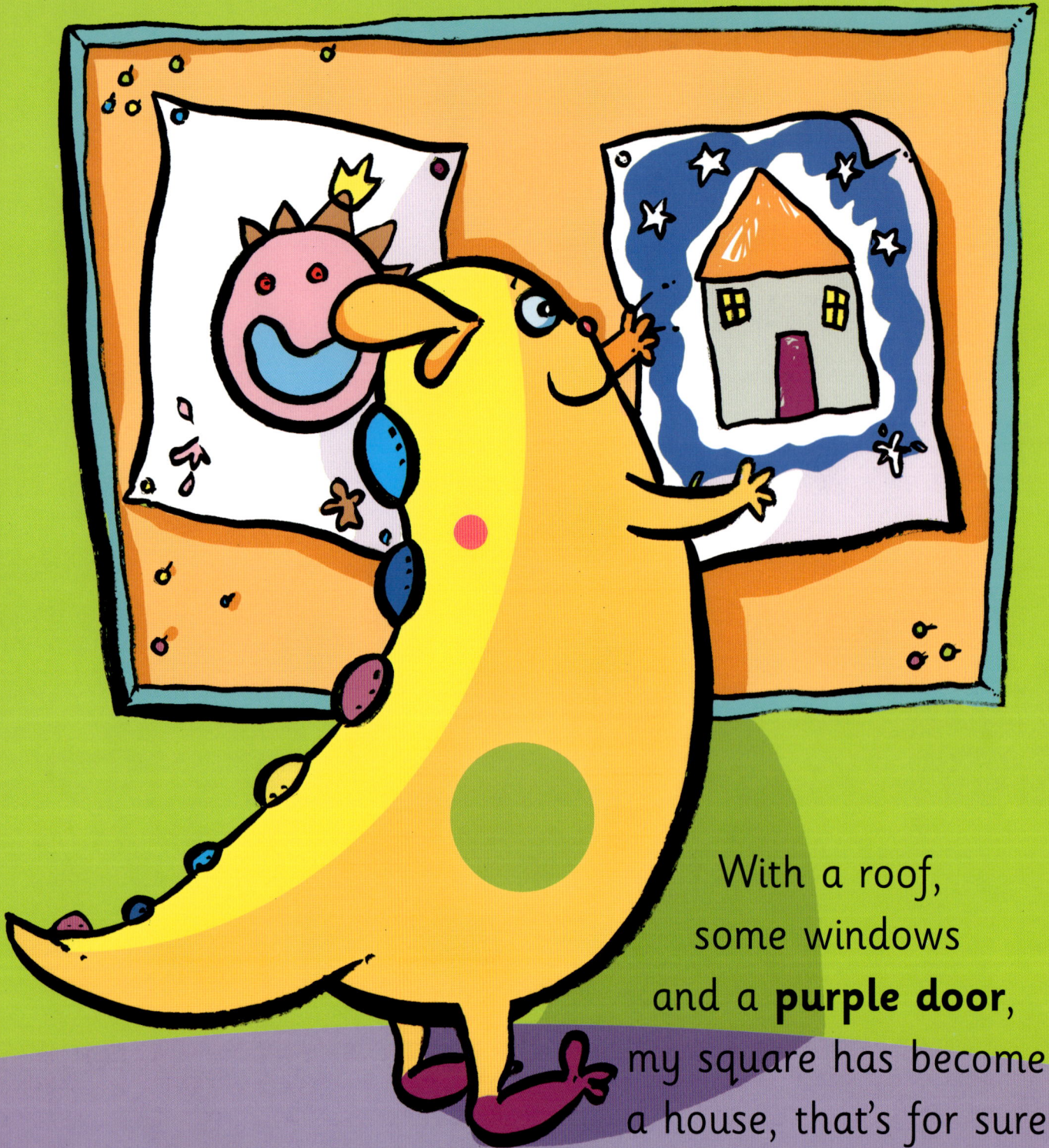

With a roof,
some windows
and a **purple door**,
my square has become
a house, that's for sure!

14

purple door

15

Now I'm drawing a shape with a **black felt pen**,
going down, then across, then up again.
Look at my drawing, there's not much to see,
but can you guess what it's going to be?

black felt pen

17

Now I've filled it with **yellow**,
red, **orange** and **green**,
it's the best jar of jelly beans
I've ever seen!

yellow
brown
red
white
pink
blue
grey
purple
green
black
orange

19

Things to do

Can you think of something that is red?

Can you think of something that is blue?

Can you think of something that is yellow?

Can you think of something that is green?

Can you think of something that is purple?

What is your favourite colour?

Things to do

How do the words for these colours begin?

Which words begin with the same sound?

Can you think of some more words that begin with these sounds?

Word bank

Colour words from the story

black

blue

brown

green

grey

orange

pink

purple

red

white

yellow

More colour words

cream

gold

mauve

scarlet

silver

turquoise

Word bank

More words from the story

 circle

 monster

 crown

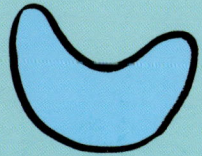 mouth

door  roof

 eyes

sky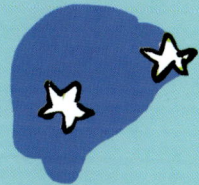

head  spike

 house

square

jar

 star

jelly beans

window

 king

23

Parents' and teachers' notes

• As you read the book to your child, run your finger along underneath the text. This will help your child to follow the reading and focus on the look of the words as well as their sound. Give your child time to respond when he or she is asked to guess what Zia is drawing.

• On the first or second reading, leave out the colour words and let your child say them. Point to the illustration to prompt an answer if necessary.

• Once your child is familiar with the book, encourage him or her to read along with you.

• Encourage your child to express opinions and preferences, e.g. 'Which of Zia's pictures do you like most? Why?' 'Which part of the book did you like best?'

• Encourage your child to think about what else he or she could draw with some basic coloured shapes. For example, 'What else could you make with a pink circle or a grey square?' 'What could you make a blue triangle into?'

• Talk about Zia and discuss the monster's appearance. Does your child think Zia is a girl or a boy? Why? (The book does not suggest one or the other.)

• Encourage your child to invent and describe a monster of his or her own. What things would the new monster like to paint?

• Draw your child's attention to the structure of some words – especially the colours. Play 'Guess the Colour' (based on 'I Spy'), e.g. 'I'm thinking of a colour and it begins with …'

• Does your child know any other colour words? Discuss how we can describe colours, i.e. from the use of words such as 'light', 'pale' and 'dark', to comparing colours to things such as 'sky blue' or 'leaf green'.

• Look at the 'Things to do' pages (pages 20–21). Read the questions to your child and help with the answers where necessary. Give your child lots of praise. Even if he or she gets an answer wrong you can say: 'That was a really good try, but it's not that one it's this one'.

• Read and discuss the words on the 'Word bank' pages (pages 22–23). Look at the letter patterns and how the words are spelled. Cover up the first part of a word and see if your child can remember what was there. See if your child can write the simpler words from memory – he or she is likely to need several attempts to write a word correctly!

• When you are talking about letter sounds, try not to add too much of an uh or er sound. Say mmm instead of muh or mer, ssss instead of suh or ser. Saying letter sounds as carefully as possible will help your child when he or she is trying to build up or spell words – rer-e-der doesn't sound much like 'red'!

• Talk about words: what they mean, how they sound, how they look and how they are spelled; but if your child gets restless or bored, stop. Enjoyment of the story, activity or book is essential if we want children to grow up valuing books and reading!

24